Just Like Music: Social Emotional Learning Inspired by Hip-Hop

David Spellmon Jr

POSITIVE ARCHER PUBLISHING

COVER AND ILLUSTRATION BY FRANCESKO ART

FOREWORD BY RITUSHREE DUTTA

ISBN: 978-1-7349237-0-4 (PAPERBACK)
ISBN: 978-1-7349237-1-1 (EBOOK)

Library of Congress Control Number: 2020909623

CONTENTS

ACKNOWLEDGEMENTS

I would first like to thank my parents David and Janet because they have instilled timeless values into our family. They continue to show me unconditional love and I wouldn't be successful without them. I especially appreciate the Motown records they blessed my ears with that started my love of music. I love you both dearly! To Marie (Girly) and Jayson, I want to make you both proud of your big brother. To Kamari, I always want to be a positive role model for you as your uncle. A special shout of peace goes out to Patrick O'Neil, who has been the best educator I have ever had in my life. You taught me that iron sharpens iron, and I try to emulate your wisdom when I mentor my students. To Dr. Lorenzo Johnson for always keeping me accountable and focused. To Roy Burton for providing me insight about the educational environment. To Shannon Weathers whose book inspired me to write my own. To Keenen Ivory Wayans for always delivering the MESSAGE! To Chuck Inglish for offering his blessing. To Ash Cash for his guidance and answering every single damn direct message that I sent him asking him about the book making process. I truly appreciate you all!

I could never forget the friends and family that I have lost. I also want to highlight the people who helped to inspire this book who are no longer here. I dedicate this book to: Marie Virginia Miller, Aunt Polly, Tony Tran, Alicia Wyman, Donnie Crenshaw, Carlos Torres, Eric Darby, Kenny Staley, Hieng "Ziggi" Chea, Kepler Charles, DeMarco Pegues, Kobe Bryant, Charlie Murphy, Lisa "Left Eye" Lopes, Marvin Gaye, Ermias Asghedom aka Nipsey Hussle, and last but not least Malik Taylor aka Phife Dawg. May you all Rest in Paradise.

FOREWORD

As a high school student, I'm sure many of you feel misunderstood and detached from the world around you. Some of you dwell in a society you have handcrafted for yourself to cope with the stresses and uncertainties of life. Some of you are disillusioned by people who tell you that there is GREATNESS INSIDE OF YOU. You are tired of waiting for that greatness to unleash itself. You are exhausted from trying to control the outcomes of your life. You try so hard every living moment of your life to be better only to encounter setbacks. Well, you are not alone.

I am Ritushree Dutta. I am just like you. I moved to the United States in 2016, which was also my freshman year at Ardrey Kell High School, Charlotte, North Carolina. As an international student, I had to learn to become comfortable with being in an environment composed of elements unfamiliar to me. Like you, I felt like I didn't belong and that I didn't have it in me to make a difference. For someone who is unforgivingly ambitious, I couldn't stand the idea of stagnation. But I am grateful for the people in my life who have shown me the GREATNESS INSIDE. One of them is Mr. David Spellmon, the author of this book, and a mentor very dear to me.

I met Mr. Spellmon over the summer of my junior year of high school at an Equity Ambassadors Program conducted by Queen City Unity. As I shyly entered the room on the first Saturday of the program, I didn't know what to expect. I was warmly greeted by Mr. Spellmon who introduced himself as the program's instructor. At first glance, Mr. Spellmon seemed to be the "chill" type of person that every student looks for. But as days went by, I came to learn that he could be as interesting when he becomes serious and philosophical when he goofs around with his students. I found myself leaving the last day of the program with something special: a new spark and a new bond.

If anything, reader, let me tell you that I am most grateful for this strong and precious bond that I share with Mr. Spellmon. I am, therefore, most excited about the bond you will soon share with him as well. Mr. Spellmon is the adult who sacrifices a weekend to attend your performance by an informal invitation you send. He is the role model who dresses-up on a commonly dressed-down day to set an example of confidence and sophistication for the black students around him. He is someone to drive through midday downtown Charlotte traffic to and from your school to participate in a 30-minute seminar you are presenting to a group of students. He is someone who puts his students before himself every step of the way because he believes in the GREATNESS THAT LIES WITHIN them.

So, why Hip-Hop? Because Mr. Spellmon knows us too well. There is a reason that he connects so profoundly with the students he works with. There is a reason his students trust him. Hip-Hop is such an integral part of our lives. The music, rhythm, and beat all work in tandem to wake us up in the morning, get us through a bad day, energize us before a competition, and hype us up at sports games. The truth is that Hip-Hop or not, the lyrics of a song truly resonate with us. Music has scientifically and historically been a powerful remedy to a broken spirit and regardless of the extent to which our lives are different today, music continues to be a powerful beacon of change. Music continues to invigorate change-makers and revolutionaries around the world and relentlessly drives us to reveal the GREATNESS WITHIN US.

My time with Mr. Spellmon has taught me so many things about myself that I will hold onto for the rest of my life. He taught me that there is a leader within me, one that wields unfathomable power to pioneer change. He showed me that there is a fighter within me, that my passion and determination towards life is key to my successes in the future. But most importantly, Mr. Spellmon helped me believe that there is GREATNESS WITHIN, a command I was born with, that is and will forever remain, true and unique to me. And I have no doubt, reader that he will show you the vast abyss of GREATNESS that belongs to YOU!

WHO **NEEDS** CHANGE? Our youth! More importantly the educators who serve our youth. The education system has provided a lack of preventive measures to help students succeed outside of academics. The focus has long been standardized testing scores and enforced compliance in regards to behavior. A study compiled data from 4,803 United States public schools found that during the 2017-18 school year, an estimated 962,300 violent incidents and 476,100 non-violent incidents occurred in US public schools nationwide. 71 percent of schools reported having at least one violent incident and 65 percent reported having at least one non-violent incident (Diliberti et al., 2019). Those numbers are already problematic but knowing that the violent incidents include: rape, sexual assault other than rape, robbery (with or without a weapon), physical attack or fight (with or without a weapon), and threat of physical attack (with or without a weapon) makes those numbers downright scary. Another reason why this change is crucial for our youth are the impacts on upward income mobility. A study looked at the odds for a child coming from the bottom 5th quintile of the national income distribution making it to the top 5th quintile in the 50 biggest cities in the United States. The bottom 10 cities have less than a six percent chance, these cities include: Indianapolis, IN (4.9), Dayton, OH (4.9), Atlanta, GA (4.5), Milwaukee, WI (4.5), and Charlotte, NC (4.4). Based on each school district's respective website, that is roughly 315,000 students! Interestingly enough, the quality of the K-12 school system and strength of an individual's social network were two of the five major factors that strongly correlated with upward mobility (Chetty et al., 2014).

WHO **WANTS** TO CHANGE? All hands down! There is no word in the English language that make educators more uncomfortable than innovation. Many K-12 schools give lip service to the concept of innovation in mission statements, on websites, in professional development trainings, during committee council and board meetings, but lose their nerve when it is time to make it happen (Heick, 2019). With that lack of innovation educators are stuck being reactive and only left with putting out the fires. Educators do not have to keep existing in this educational purgatory that either leads to burnout and career changes or years of unhappiness until they retire. There is an abundance of research highlighting the positive effects of interventions geared towards the Collaborative for Academic, Social, and Emotional Learning (CASEL) five core competencies which are: SELF-AWARENESS, SELF-MANAGEMENT, SOCIAL AWARENESS, RELATIONSHIP SKILLS, and RESPONSIBLE DECISION-MAKING. Students with strong social and emotional skills are also more likely to initiate and sustain positive relationships with peers and adults, participate in classroom activities, and engage in learning (Jones, Barnes, Bailey, & Doolittle, 2017; Greenberg et al., 2017; Durlak et al., 2011; Farrington et al., 2012; Sklad et al., 2012; Weissberg et al., 2015; Denham, 2006). Building social and emotional skills and competencies also has important value from a public-health perspective. Universal school-based programs focused on these skills have the capacity to influence short and long-term physical and mental health outcomes for all children. By facilitating the development of skills such as how to manage emotions, such interventions can serve as important protective factors and change the way individuals adapt to their environment and respond to stress (Greenberg, Katz, & Klein, 2015; Buckner, Mezzacappa, & Beardslee, 2003,2009). Likewise, the inability to cope effectively with stress or regulate one's emotions is associated with numerous diseases that influence the physiological response system (Greenberg et al., 2015). This is particularly relevant for children exposed to chronic stress often associated with poverty, violence, and substance abuse, conditions that have long-lasting consequences for learning, behavior, and general physical and mental well-being (Center on the Developing Child, 2007; Thompson, 2014).

WHO WANTS TO **LEAD** THE CHANGE? This is where I come in! One big concept we talk about in K-12 education is ensuring our students gain 21st Century Skills, they are important to helping students keep up with the pace of today's job market. The four C's coined the "Learning Skills" are essential because they are needed in any career. Critical Thinking, Creativity, Collaboration, and Communication are the most popular of the 21st Century Skills (Stauffer, 2020). The four C's remind me of key themes in another concept we have discussed, Social Emotional Learning! Critical Thinking or problem solving goes hand in hand with RESPONSIBLE DECISION-MAKING, analyzing situations to make the most appropriate decision and being ethical. Creativity is all about SELF-AWARENESS, having the self-confidence to do things differently and be innovative. Collaboration please meet SOCIAL AWARENESS; appreciating diversity, showing empathy, and having respect for others are important to completing any task within a group. Communication is all about RELATIONSHIP SKILLS, more importantly effective communication will improve both your relationships and teamwork with others.

Creating more engaged and positive students in the classroom. Check. Better physical and mental health. Check. Adapting to change and effectively dealing with stress, especially important for the students they love to label as "troubled", or having "Attention Deficit Disorder" and "Oppositional Defiant Disorder".

3

Check. Preparing them for life in today's job environment. Check. It seems like every student in the nation would benefit from engaging in constant Social Emotional Learning activities. How is this conversation on Social Emotional Learning any different from the current ones taking place in the education sector? Like Marvin sang, "Just like the Music!" The integration of Hip-Hop Music, but not simply listening to the music, we will break down lyrics to find the Social Emotional Learning gems dropped! When you drop gems you are sharing useful knowledge or information with others. The five core competencies are like muscles and we all know the more you train a muscle the stronger it becomes. The knowledge you will get from these lyrics will finely tune your Social Emotional muscles without the gym membership, it only requires an individual with an open mindset and the drive to improve.

To be fair, some Hip-Hop music does have explicit language and negative references in them, but Hip-Hop can also offer positivity and Social Emotional Learning lessons if you know how to look! Each lyric chosen is special to me because it has provided motivation, guidance, and positive energy to me throughout the years. These lyrics have also allowed me to help others get through difficult situations. Get familiar with the phrase YOU HAVE GREATNESS INSIDE OF YOU! It is there from the day you are born, and it is the theme of this book! This book was designed to be a resource to engage those students who get overlooked because of their discipline issues, who feel like school is not for them, and who may not have positive individuals in their lives. I want this book to serve as a pivotal tool to show students their unique gifts by understanding their self-identity, building their resilience, and being a constant reminder that they are powerful. By offering up Social Emotional Learning lessons found in Hip-Hop, I am creating an innovative way to teach these skills by meeting students in a space they are very familiar with. Additionally, there are Common Core State Standards for English Language Arts integrated into every lesson. I recommend that staff read the entire book and complete each of the activities prior to facilitating with their students to display the restorative approach of engaging in this process with students. Lastly, real connections will take place and bonds will be formed because this program when done with fidelity will create community, and the opportunity for a student's identity (Hip-Hop culture) to be accepted into their education, when it has always been told to stay at home. I hope you are ready to embark on this Social Emotional musical journey as we experience 14 unique destinations that will promote major personal growth for both students and the individuals that interact with them.

PHILADELPHIA, PA

The first set of lyrics in this musical Social Emotional Learning journey are powerful! It is only right that we visit the City of Brotherly Love. Welcome to Philadelphia, Pennsylvania, and this will be the beginning of our personal renaissance. Not only have these lyrics been featured as an impromptu fight song for the Philadelphia Eagles during their 2017 season that ended in a Super Bowl victory. These lyrics have also been a source of inspiration and motivation for me ever since I was introduced to them in 2012. All I need is the opening line to take my mind to a higher level, "I used to pray for times like this, to rhyme like this so I had to grind like that to shine like this."[1] If you know the song you can feel the energy coming from the intro. This is your first of many reminders that **YOU HAVE GREATNESS INSIDE OF YOU!**

I am a student of the *7 Habits of Highly Effective People* (Covey, 1989) and Habit 2 discusses that all things are created twice. The greatness that I am speaking about is your aura, and it is something that cannot be seen initially. It is the vision you have of yourself and the things you are going to accomplish, and most importantly it is the first creation. The second creation is the physical manifestation and that is the actual work you put into making the vision your reality! Going back to the lyrics, the artist is telling you that he has engaged both creations and is now reaping his rewards. Correct me if I am wrong, but people pray about the things they want but do not have yet, their dreams and such are the first creation. When you leave your comfort zone to go after your goal, constantly practice or study, and the long days are over you get the desired results. The recognition that comes from that hard work is when you have completed the second creation.

Your SELF-MANAGEMENT muscles are being worked to fuel the entire process of taking your vision to fruition. First you must create the goals you want to achieve, then stay disciplined and keep your motivation levels high until you complete them. A major piece to this concept is believing in yourself, and maintaining a positive self-identity. You are worthy and capable of achieving all that you set out to accomplish! You control your effort! You control what you allow your attention to be on! You must also Trust the Process! If it were easy, everyone would be on the honor roll, be a champion, or have that top position. When you are on your grind, luck and success seem to come your way! Hold up wait a minute, y'all thought I was finished?

LESSON PLAN FOR PHILADELPHIA

Materials Needed: Poster boards, magazines, pens, markers or pencils, student's workbooks, and a computer with internet access.

Objective: Students will train their SELF-MANAGEMENT muscles by constructing a vision board that illustrates the 1st creation concept. Students will also create one detailed plan for an academic and a personal goal. (**Skill – GOAL SETTING**)

CCSS.ELA: RL.9-10.1 Cite strong and thorough textual evidence to support analysis of what the text says explicitly as well as inferences drawn from the text. RL.9-10.2 Determine a theme of a text and analyze in detail its development over the course of the text, including how it emerges and is shaped and refined by specific details; provide an objective summary of the text. RL.9-10.9 Analyze how an author draws on and transforms source material in a specific work. SL.9-10.1 Initiate and participate effectively in a range of collaborative discussions (one-on-one, in groups, and teacher-led) with diverse partners on grades 9–10 topics, texts, and issues, building on others' ideas and expressing their own clearly and persuasively.

Appetizer: What is the theme of this text?

Vocabulary: The instructor will review the vocabulary words. The instructor will ask for examples of each vocabulary word. Goal- The end towards which effort is directed. Fruition- Attainment of anything desired. Motivation- The state or condition of being motivated or having a strong reason to act or accomplish something. On your grind- Working hard. Renaissance- A rebirth, the act of changing in a positive way. Visualize- Form a mental image of, imagine.

Prior Knowledge: The instructor will play the video of the Philadelphia Eagles winning Super Bowl 52. YouTube: "Philly's Celebration After Final Play & the Gatorade Shower! | Eagles vs. Patriots | Super Bowl LII" https://youtu.be/7TZ_2rIGYLE. The instructor will ask students to predict the emotions they would show in that moment, for the winning and losing side.

New Knowledge: The instructor will remind students that before any person or team achieves their goal, they first had a vision of it! That's the 1st creation. It is like seeing into the future! The 2nd creation is the hard work that goes into bringing the 1st creation to reality. You never see all the work that went into the success, but without motivation and working hard there can be no success. Give students 3-5 minutes to jot down some goals to implement onto their vision boards.

Guided Practice: Creating a Vision Board. The instructor will create a vision board along with the students (or have a premade vision board to show students). The instructor will share the items from their vision board. Students will document academic and personal goals through pictures and words on their vision boards. Students can illustrate or post pictures from magazines or the internet onto their boards. The instructor will lead a call and response chant with the students at the conclusion of the activity: The instructor will say 1st creation and instruct the students to respond, vision. The instructor will say 2nd creation and instruct the students to respond, work. This will happen a few times then the instructor will hold up 1 finger and students will say vision, when the instructor holds up 2 fingers the students will say work.

Independent Practice: Students will assess and choose one academic and one personal goal from their vision board and generate the 2nd creation steps needed to achieve the goal. Students will work independently. The instructor will share the example: If the goal is to make the honor roll, some actionable steps could be reducing time on social media to study, have no missing classroom or homework assignments, study for 30 minutes a day, going to tutoring sessions, etc. Look at the bigger picture, who else will be affected by the student's completion of the goal? Students will share with the class one goal and the steps needed to achieve it. For the student's academic goals, the instructor will make copies to keep at school to have them frequently review during the school day. You have now become their Accountability Coach.

Lesson Wrap Up: Students will answer what is the 1st Creation? 2nd Creation? What do you need to achieve any goal? Students will document responses in their workbook, instruct students to cite textual evidence from the passage. Students will share out.

*Challenge: Identify lyrics in a song that you like that gets you motivated, the lyrics must be clean!

Ibiza, SPAIN

We now travel to a popular island off the coast of Spain! When I first started writing this book, I envisioned my target audience being middle and high school students. The more I wrote I realized that these lyrics and messages can benefit any person that wants to increase their Social-Emotional skills. You all know how much I love this phrase, but even in the down times remember that **YOU HAVE GREATNESS INSIDE OF YOU!** I say that to say this, sooner or later everyone will unfortunately experience a heartbreak, from the 2nd grader whose crush doesn't like them back to individuals getting divorced after many years of marriage.

The following lyric is very personal to me. "I've been down, I've been low, had my mattress on the floor"[2] takes me back to a difficult time in my life. I was coming off a bad breakup where we were living together, and I had to move out of my girlfriend's apartment. I had to find a place of my own and I literally had nothing in my new place but an air mattress for the first few months. I spent many nights looking up at the ceiling, and those were not the best of times. In moments like that people generally move in two ways: we sink into a dark place where pity parties are thrown **or** we acknowledge the pain but we know we must move on. I still had to go to work and be productive, and feeling sorry for myself was not an option.

For my students, as a result of a breakup I know you will feel shame and embarrassment going back to school and seeing that person. This is when an individual must develop and grow their SELF-AWARENESS, SELF-MANAGEMENT and RESPONSIBLE DECISION-MAKING muscles. Reflecting is always a good intervention whether you journal your thoughts, engage in positive self-talk or speak to a friend. The SELF-AWARENESS to know that yes, I am hurting right now, but life will go on and you are so much more than your relationship status. Making constructive choices is key to finding new outlets to get oneself in a better place. As for my story, I was able to get through that rough period of time with the help of exercising my Social-Emotional muscles while leaning on friends and family. You must tap into your optimism as well to know that there will be better days ahead. These same skills can be used for all types of setbacks and disappointments, not just for getting through a breakup (**MESSAGE!**). This is an important part, causing that individual pain since they caused you pain is never the answer. Do not try to retaliate through seeking revenge, it is an unproductive way to handle any situation. Your "revenge" will be no revenge. Find joy in moving forward with your life and becoming a better person.

LESSON PLAN FOR IBIZA

Materials Needed: Flip chart paper, markers, pens or pencils, and student's workbooks.

Objective: Students will train their SELF-MANAGEMENT muscles by designing a list of positive coping skills specifically tailored for them. Students will role play their coping skills in a safe space to familiarize themselves with the techniques. (**Skill – STRESS MANAGEMENT**)

CCSS.ELA: RL.9-10.1 Cite strong and thorough textual evidence to support analysis of what the text says explicitly as well as inferences drawn from the text. RL.9-10.2 Determine a theme of a text and analyze in detail its development over the course of the text, including how it emerges and is shaped and refined by specific details; provide an objective summary of the text. W.9-10.3 Write narratives to develop real or imagined experiences or events using effective technique, well-chosen details, and well-structured event sequences. SL.9-10.1 Initiate and participate effectively in a range of collaborative discussions (one-on-one, in groups, and teacher-led) with diverse partners on grades 9–10 topics, texts, and issues, building on others' ideas and expressing their own clearly and persuasively.

Appetizer: What is the theme of this text?

Vocabulary: The instructor will review the vocabulary words. The instructor will ask for examples of each vocabulary word. Constructive- Serving to improve or advance. Coping Skills- The methods a person uses to deal with stressful situations. Critical Thinking- The analysis of facts to form a judgment. Stress- A physical, chemical, or emotional factor that causes bodily or mental tension.

Prior Knowledge- The instructor will ask students to recall a time where they experienced a disappointment, or setback. Students will reflect about their feelings in that moment. Examples: My parent said this but..., I thought I did well on a test but..., my friend told my secret about..., etc. The instructor should share a personal story.

New Knowledge- The instructor will inform students that they have been using Coping Skills all their lives, some positive and some negative. Physical: positive-engaging in an active body drill or working out, negative- fighting or causing self-harm. Support: positive- talking to a trusted friend or adult, negative- speaking to instigators or making a social media post when upset.

Guided Practice: List of Coping Skills. Students will compare constructive vs. destructive ways to deal with a situation on flip chart paper. The instructor along with students will create a list of both positive and negative coping skills. If there is a disagreement on a coping skill, students will debate on why it should be positive or negative. Students will also differentiate coping skills for use at school and at home. The bigger the list, the better for the independent practice activity. The instructor will highlight consequences of positive and negative coping skills.

Independent Practice: Students will select a list of three (3) coping skills that they feel will work for them. Students will then role play a scenario of them engaging in one of their coping skills successfully.

Lesson Wrap Up: Students will compose a narrative about utilizing their coping skills. Students will have to explain the situations that are causing them stress, why they chose the coping skill, and how it is constructive (why it's positive versus negative). Students will document responses in their workbook, instruct students to cite textual evidence from the passage. Students will share out.

*****Challenge**: Identify lyrics in a song that you like that talk about positive coping skills, the lyrics must be clean!

DETROIT, MI

"I never really met nobody who was truly successful that wasn't thankful."[3] These words set the stage for the RELATIONSHIP SKILL muscle building that will take place in this lyrical analysis as we visit the birthplace of Motown, Detroit, Michigan. I always tell people when you send good vibes out to the world a lot of times they come right back! Establishing and maintaining healthy relationships are vital to the concept here. The lyric embodies gratitude. We often forget or overlook the people in our lives that have helped us achieve success, but claim it was all self-made. That success a person experiences is going to look differently across the board, but the point being, we need to acknowledge those who contributed to helping us achieve it. Sometimes saying thank you goes a long way because appreciating a person is an anomaly these days but let's go deeper. Imagine the joy a person will have when they receive a gratitude letter from someone who has not forgotten about the good energy that was given to them. It could be a parent, grandparent, teacher, coach, mentor, friend, or anybody really and it could bring the strongest person to tears.

Another angle I want to convey is being gracious towards waking up each day. YOU HAVE GREATNESS INSIDE OF YOU! Once you realize that, you become your own movement and in every moment, you must take actions that will lead to success today. I encourage you all to embrace living in the present moment. We cannot change the past and the future is determined by what we do right now! Another lyric from this song where the artist raps "And I'm right here, right now, how could I not give thanks?"[3] Resonates deeply in my soul because there were a few situations where I could have lost my life. I experienced a near drowning situation and had someone pull a gun on a friend and I but the gun jammed. I know I'm not the only person who feels like there is a reason they are on this Earth. There are many people who do lose their lives on a daily basis, but you are stressing over a few bad seconds, minutes, or hours? Be grateful for the opportunity to overcome those things! We all will go through down moments in our lives but that is when those relationships you have built pay dividends. When you are good to people they cannot wait to return the favor when you need it (MESSAGE!). The more good energy you send out the stronger your legacy will be. As Maya Angelou stated "People often will forget the things you have said to them, but they will never forget the way you made them feel."

LESSON PLAN FOR DETROIT

Materials Needed: Pens, markers or pencils, student's workbooks, and a computer with internet access.

Objective: Students will train their RELATIONSHIP SKILL muscles by interpreting the thematic elements of the lyrical breakdown by creating gratitude letters for family members or friends. (**Skill – RELATIONSHIP BUILDING**)

CCSS.ELA: RL.9-10.1 Cite strong and thorough textual evidence to support analysis of what the text says explicitly as well as inferences drawn from the text. RL.9-10.2 Determine a theme of a text and analyze in detail its development over the course of the text, including how it emerges and is shaped and refined by specific details; provide an objective summary of the text. W.9-10.3 Write narratives to develop real or imagined experiences or events using effective technique, well-chosen details, and well-structured event sequences. SL.9-10. Initiate and participate effectively in a range of collaborative discussions (one-on-one, in groups, and teacher-led) with diverse partners on grades 9–10 topics, texts, and issues, building on others' ideas and expressing their own clearly and persuasively. SL.9-10.4 Present information, findings, and supporting evidence clearly, concisely, and logically such that listeners can follow the line of reasoning and the organization, development, substance, and style are appropriate to purpose, audience, and task.

Appetizer: What is the theme of this text?

Vocabulary: The instructor will review the vocabulary words. The instructor will ask for examples of each vocabulary word. Anomaly- Something different, abnormal. Gratitude- The quality of being grateful or thankful. Relationship- The way in which two or more concepts, objects, or people are connected. Resonate- To produce a positive feeling or emotional response.

Prior Knowledge- The instructor will ask students how they create and maintain friendships. The instructor will then ask students how they express gratitude to the people they care about.

14

New Knowledge- The instructor will monitor the student's level of gratitude towards waking up today and ask them how they feel on a scale of 0-10 (0- no gratitude, 10 extreme gratitude). The instructor will encourage students not to take advantage of the days they are given and to do their best everyday.

Guided Practice: The instructor will play Kevin Durant's MVP speech. YouTube: "Kevin Durant delivers famous 'You the Real MVP' 2014 NBA MVP acceptance speech | ESPN Archives" https://youtu.be/MN5YnVlDnIQ. Students will compare the gratitude Kevin Durant gave to the individuals he thanked during his speech. Students will document the person and how Kevin Durant expressed his gratitude. Students will share out.

Independent Practice: I Thank You! Students will create a list of people who they consider a mentor, coach, mother or father figure, or a positive person they look up to. (Note, this can be a family member). Students will write a gratitude letter to one of those individuals explaining why they are writing them the letter, all the things they have done for them, the encouraging words they have given, how they made them feel special, etc.

Lesson Wrap Up: Students will answer why expressing gratitude is important? Students will document responses in their workbook, instruct students to cite textual evidence from the passage. Students will share out.

*Challenges: Identify lyrics in a song that you like that expresses gratitude, the lyrics must be clean! Write another gratitude letter to a different individual.

*Bonus: This activity is optional but will be powerful if students choose to participate. Students will record themselves reading their gratitude letter to their person and will present to the group. Students will reflect on the experience during the next session.

BROOKLYN, NY

We head to the Brooklyn borough for the next two lessons. It is the second most densely populated county in the United States! The lyric from this Hip-Hop track helped me learn one of the most valuable lessons in my life, whether you want to call it accountability or self-reflection. If you have ever had the pleasure of going to a Southern Baptist church this line will be too familiar. Often the pastor will say while preaching "now some of y'all ain't gonna like me today, but can I preach this thing right now?" When any preacher communicates that line you know they are about to speak truth to a subject that most people do not want to acknowledge. While this preacher who is hilariously played by Charlie Murphy does not prepare the audience with that line the parallels are still there because he is speaking to a truth that most people still struggle with. Pastor Charlie Murphy talks about a certain type of individual who hates change and hates progress. He further describes this type of individual as hating their own mother because they think it is her fault that they do not have success. Pastor Charlie Murphy then delivers the line that will be the focus on this lyrical breakdown, "YOU are the architect of your own misery."[4]

It takes some serious SELF-AWARENESS and RESPONSIBLE DECISION-MAKING to hear that line and connect with it immediately. When you have experienced a failure or things did not go the way you wanted, how many times did you take an introspective look? Did you focus on the things you have done or did not do that led to the outcome or did you blame everything else? There have been many times where I have said to myself that I have made a bad outcome happen by my actions. You all know me by now so let me kindly remind you that YOU HAVE GREATNESS INSIDE OF YOU! You can be the architect of your success!

You must have perspective, so you can see the errors of your ways and correct them. You must maintain the belief that you can succeed or make it right even when you mess up. When your mindset is you are the architect of your own success you hold yourself accountable and there are no longer opportunities to blame outside forces for you not achieving the goal. This also speaks to not being too down on yourself either. You will not win 100% of the time nor achieve every goal on the first try. It becomes a good self-challenge when you must tap into your inner strength to reach success. The wise person once said that victory is most satisfying when you have known defeat.

LESSON PLAN FOR BROOKLYN

Materials Needed: Pens or pencils, Flip chart paper, and student's workbooks.

Objective: Students will train their RESPONSIBLE DECISION-MAKING muscles by selecting strategies that will produce an increase in constructive choices. (SKILLS – EVALUATING AND REFLECTING)

CCSS.ELA: RL.9-10.1 Cite strong and thorough textual evidence to support analysis of what the text says explicitly as well as inferences drawn from the text. RL.9-10.2 Determine a theme of a text and analyze in detail its development over the course of the text, including how it emerges and is shaped and refined by specific details; provide an objective summary of the text. W.9-10.3 Write narratives to develop real or imagined experiences or events using effective technique, well-chosen details, and well-structured event sequences. SL.9-10.1 Initiate and participate effectively in a range of collaborative discussions (one-on-one, in groups, and teacher-led) with diverse partners on grades 9–10 topics, texts, and issues, building on others' ideas and expressing their own clearly and persuasively.

Appetizer: What is the theme of this text?

Vocabulary: The instructor will review the vocabulary words. The instructor will ask for examples of each vocabulary word. Accountable- Responsible for and having to explain your actions. Architect- A person who designs and guides a plan or undertaking. Evaluate- To judge the quality, importance, amount, or value of something. Introspection- An examination of one's own thoughts and feelings. Reflect- To think carefully, especially about possibilities and opinions. Success- The accomplishment of an aim or purpose.

Prior Knowledge- The instructor will ask students to raise their hands if they have ever blamed someone else for them getting in trouble, not making a good grade, or forgetting to do something. The instructor will offer the examples: they called me a name so I hit them and the teachers don't teach. The instructor will then ask students to raise their hands again if they ever blamed someone else when things went right for them. The instructor will offer examples of making a good grade or getting complimented for doing a good deed. The instructor will state that they do not blame others for their good decisions!

New Knowledge- The instructor will inform students that they are the same person, but the decisions they make changes. The instructor will encourage students to be humble when good decisions get made and to be accountable when bad decisions get made.

Guided Practice: The instructor along with students will create scenarios on flip chart paper to investigate if the individual took accountability or not. Students can be in pairs or groups. Example: A student forgot to set their alarm to wake up for the bus, their parent works third shift has to wake up and rush to take them to school but there is traffic which causes the student to be extremely late. The student yells at his parent, blames them for being late and slams the car door. The instructor will ask who is at fault, the possible consequences, and how the harm can be repaired.

Independent Practice: Students will reflect on one of their limitations or problem behaviors. Students will then create a scenario where they have taken their limitation or problem behavior and became the architect of their success. Students will share the positive consequences of their behavior change. Students will share out with the group.

Lesson Wrap Up: Students will define architect and success. Students will then document a plan to reach their success in their workbook.

*Challenge: Identify lyrics in a song that you like that talks about accountability, the lyrics must be clean!

BED-STUY, BROOKLYN

The following lyric focuses on building our RESPONSIBLE DECISION-MAKING muscles, "Beef is only good when you're in the burger business."[5] One of the greatest Hip-Hop artists of all time, Biggie Smalls, enlightened us back in 1997 of this concept with "What's Beef?" Beef is essentially an ongoing problem between two individuals or two groups of people. Beef potentially puts not only you in danger but the people you care about as well because the other side might hurt them to hurt you. Beef has caused many people to make life changing decisions as a result of misunderstandings that have severe consequences. Remember the statistic from the introduction, an estimated 962,300 violent incidents occurred during the 2017-18 school year. The message is clear, if you are not the master griller at the cookout then you should not be engaging in beef.

Let me further explore this concept. The brain is the intellect and the heart is the emotion, and in any normal situation our intellect rules over our emotions but in situations where we feel we have been wronged, or get extremely upset, they flip flop. When we allow our emotions to overtake our intellect, we then make poor choices. Even when you are upset, you are still in control of your actions. Never forget that you can always improve because **YOU HAVE GREATNESS INSIDE OF YOU!** I encourage everyone reading this book to work on building your equanimity muscles as well. Inner strength is essential to analyzing a situation and knowing there is power from stepping away from a conflict. Do not allow petty things or the peer pressure of others to consume you because beef never results in a positive consequence. Another thing to focus on is the people you keep around you. If they are always getting into conflicts then they will drag you into their beefs too (**MESSAGE!**). I do want to offer you some food for thought, a job will never ask you in an interview how many fights have you won, therefore engaging in beef should not be worn around like a badge of honor.

LESSON PLAN FOR BED-STUY

Materials Needed: Dominoes, student's workbooks, and pens or pencils.

Objective: Students will train their RESPONSIBLE DECISION-MAKING muscles by determining the potential consequences of being in control versus not being in control. (**Skill – ANALYZING SITUATIONS**)

CCSS.ELA: RL.9-10.2 Determine a theme of a text and analyze in detail its development over the course of the text, including how it emerges and is shaped and refined by specific details; provide an objective summary of the text. W.9-10.3 Write narratives to develop real or imagined experiences or events using effective technique, well-chosen details, and well-structured event sequences. SL.9-10.1 Initiate and participate effectively in a range of collaborative discussions (one-on-one, in groups, and teacher-led) with diverse partners on grades 9–10 topics, texts, and issues, building on others' ideas and expressing their own clearly and persuasively.

Appetizer: What is the theme of this text?

Vocabulary: The instructor will review the vocabulary words. The instructor will ask for examples of each vocabulary word. Analyze- To examine carefully and in detail so as to identify causes, key factors, possible results, etc. Consequence- A result or effect of an action or condition. Equanimity- Mental calmness, composure, and evenness of temper, especially in a difficult situation. Petty- Little importance, trivial.

Prior Knowledge- The instructor will ask students to reflect on how their anger issues have gotten them into trouble in the past. Each student will share out.

New Knowledge- The instructor will ask students if they were ever rewarded for getting into a conflict. The instructor will communicate that everyone gets angry but it's how you handle the emotion that will determine how many "beefs" you will encounter.

Guided Practice: Domino Effect. The instructor along with the students will line up dominoes in a pattern of their choice. Students will knock over one domino and witness all the dominoes fall down. The instructor will compare the chain reaction of the dominoes to a conflict. An example to use: students were talking negatively about each other on social media, one student threatens to fight once he sees the other student at school, people hype up the situation, the students fight and both receive suspensions, the conflict carries over to the neighborhood, and someone's house gets shot up. The instructor will encourage students to think of the consequences that both families will experience as a result of the conflict. The students will line up the dominoes again but this time the instructor will remove one close to the starting point. Students will knock over the first domino and this time only a few fall down, hence the power of removing yourself from a conflict. The instructor will engage students in a discussion to reflect on the activity.

Independent Practice: Students will complete their I over E worksheet. One picture will show the brain over the heart (Intellect over Emotions) the students will document how they would decrease the tensions verbally when they are in control and predict the resolution. The second picture will depict the heart over the brain (Emotions over Intellect) the student will now predict what kind of language they would be using when they are emotional and not thinking. Students will hypothesize the conflicts that could come from the negative interactions.

Lesson Wrap Up: Students will explain the power of stepping away from a conflict in their own words. Students will document responses in their workbook.

*Challenge: Identify lyrics in a song that you like that highlights conflict resolution, the lyrics must be clean!

New Orleans, LA

We now touch down in a city with a rich history and a mélange of cultures. New Orleans is home to Jazz, Blues, Rock n Roll, Mardi Gras, Voodoo, and the Louisiana Purchase! The lyric "You either build or destroy"[6] speaks to our SOCIAL AWARENESS and RELATIONSHIP SKILL muscles. Let us all recognize the GREATNESS in others by being respectful to them. People often forget that being nice does not cost you a thing and it can actually serve you in the long run. When you show respect to others, engage in positive interactions, and are consistent; there is a great chance that people will speak highly of you and you never know what kind of opportunities that can lead to. This kind of behavior also expands your social capital because people who you have shared a positive experience with will want to introduce you to others with good energy.

One of my favorite concepts in life is connecting the dots. This is the ability to find what things people share or have in common versus stating the obvious differences. That is key to building a relationship of any type. The things I say to or about people, will help to build some sort of relationship or ensure it will not be a positive one, and the same goes for my actions. I have heard many stories about people missing out on opportunities because they talked about or treated someone badly. You never know who people may know and you do not want negative energy associated with your name. This lyric speaks to every interaction you have with someone, so you have the power to build a solid relationship or destroy one. Do not allow your perception of someone to get you in trouble either. A wise person once told me that you treat the janitor with the same respect you treat the CEO (MESSAGE!).

I am encouraging people to start sending out good energy but understand this, just because you send out good energy it may not come back in the same way. There is a quote by Paul Auster that illustrates that point, "Good begets good; evil begets evil; and even if the good you give is met by evil, you have no choice but to go on giving better than you get." Your life will be the result of the decisions you have made. Do not become an individual who gossips and treats people badly, because things can change in an instant and when the shoe is on the other foot people will remember how you treated them. Remember that YOU HAVE GREATNESS INSIDE OF YOU! Therefore, the actions you show and energy you send out should be great as well!

LESSON PLAN FOR NEW ORLEANS

Materials Needed: Small handheld mirrors, pens or pencils, and student's workbooks.

Objective: Students will train their RELATIONSHIP SKILL muscles in a communication activity designed to improve their interactions with their peers and adults. (SKILLS – COMMUNICATION AND RELATIONSHIP BUILDING)

CCSS.ELA: RL.9-10.1 Cite strong and thorough textual evidence to support analysis of what the text says explicitly as well as inferences drawn from the text. RL.9-10.2 Determine a theme of a text and analyze in detail its development over the course of the text, including how it emerges and is shaped and refined by specific details; provide an objective summary of the text. W.9-10.3 Write narratives to develop real or imagined experiences or events using effective technique, well-chosen details, and well-structured event sequences. SL.9-10.1 Initiate and participate effectively in a range of collaborative discussions (one-on-one, in groups, and teacher-led) with diverse partners on grades 9–10 topics, texts, and issues, building on others' ideas and expressing their own clearly and persuasively.

Appetizer: What is the theme of this text?

Vocabulary: The instructor will review the vocabulary words. The instructor will ask for examples of each vocabulary word. Communication- The symbolic, verbal, or written exchange of information. Golden Rule- Treat others the way you want to be treated. Hostile- Unfriendly (environment). Perception- A belief or opinion often held based on how things seem. Respect-Admiration for someone that you believe has good qualities. Social Capital- The network of relationships among people who live and work in a society.

Prior Knowledge- The instructor will ask students if they have had someone talk about them in a negative way? Ask if anyone wants to share that experience, focus on the feelings. The instructor will then ask students if they have ever talked about someone in a negative way.

26

New Knowledge- The instructor will remind students that building or destroying a relationship is based on the things they say or do to others. The instructor will give the scenario: student A spreads gossip about student B but doesn't know that student B works at and their father is the manager of the store Student A is applying to. Could this decrease student A's chances of getting a job? Why?

Guided Practice: The instructor will allow students to think, pair, share to create two scenarios: one where they will identify strategies to help build a good relationship and one where their actions helped to destroy a relationship. Students will share out to the entire group. The instructor will help students to brainstorm different scenarios.

Independent Practice: Mirror, Mirror! The instructor will give every student a mirror for this activity. Students will hold the mirror up while saying negative things to themselves to recreate them talking badly about someone else. The instructor will state that this is what it looks like when they are talking about someone. The instructor will then allow students to reflect on the activity by writing down how they felt looking at themselves say hurtful things.

Lesson Wrap Up: Students will form a sequential restorative circle and communicate how they can improve their positive interactions with peers. Students will document responses in their workbook.

*Challenge: Identify lyrics in a song that you like that talk about building up others, the lyrics must be clean!

LOS ANGELES, CA

We travel halfway across the country to the City of Angels also known as Los Angeles, California. This technically does not come from a Hip-Hop song, but Rhythm and Blues (R&B) is part of the family and Social Emotional lessons can be found in all genres of music. When I first heard "Pain" by Jhene Aiko I automatically thought about all my female friends that have gone through similar situations. Now I want to empower all people when they are feeling like they are not being treated the way they should be in a relationship.

Actions will always tell the true story (**MESSAGE!**), stop allowing words to paint a false sense of a perfect relationship. We are working our SELF-AWARENESS muscles with this track. You cannot allow someone to downplay your emotions. If something feels off, then you should be able to speak on it without getting dismissed. When you know your worth it allows you to move on from a bad situation because you know you deserve more than what you are currently getting. You will be ok removing yourself from a toxic situation, how do I know you will be ok? **YOU HAVE GREATNESS INSIDE OF YOU!** We need to practice being more kind to ourselves on a daily basis. If we do not feel good and secure internally then we think we deserve the bad treatment we may receive, and that is unacceptable. Also, when you don't think highly of yourself it impacts all areas of your life. Your work suffers, you are frustrated by everything, and you end up pushing people away. Evaluate and realign your goals to the types of things that serve you. You are too blessed to be stressed! Surround yourself with people who care about you and who want to help you grow. Focus on building an accurate self-perception of yourself to know that you are a good one and you will successfully move on from anyone who did not appreciate you.

LESSON PLAN FOR LOS ANGELES

Materials Needed: Pens or pencils and student's workbooks.

Objective: Students will train their SELF-AWARENESS muscles by deconstructing the message of a self-love quote and identifying strategies to boost the way they feel about themselves. (**Skill – ACCURATE SELF-PERCEPTION**)

CCSS.ELA: RL.9-10.1 Cite strong and thorough textual evidence to support analysis of what the text says explicitly as well as inferences drawn from the text. RL.9-10.2 Determine a theme of a text and analyze in detail its development over the course of the text, including how it emerges and is shaped and refined by specific details; provide an objective summary of the text. W.9-10.3 Write narratives to develop real or imagined experiences or events using effective technique, well-chosen details, and well-structured event sequences. SL.9-10.1 Initiate and participate effectively in a range of collaborative discussions (one-on-one, in groups, and teacher-led) with diverse partners on grades 9–10 topics, texts, and issues, building on others' ideas and expressing their own clearly and persuasively.

Appetizer: What is the theme of this text?

Vocabulary: The instructor will review the vocabulary words. The instructor will ask for examples of each vocabulary word. Affirmation- Positive and uplifting statement you say to yourself. Emotion- A natural instinctive state of mind deriving from one's circumstances, mood, or relationships with others. Inequality- The quality of being unfair or uneven. Intuition- An ability to understand or know something immediately based on your feelings rather than facts. Self-Perception- a person's view of themselves or of any of the mental or physical attributes that constitute the self.

Prior Knowledge- The instructor will ask students if they have ever been unhappy in a friendship or relationship. The instructor will then ask students if they were unhappy with the person or themselves for allowing certain things to happen.

30

Guided Practice: The instructor will present students with the quote "Love yourself first, because that's who you'll be spending the rest of your life with." The instructor will ask students to analyze what the quote means to them. The instructor along with the students will share their thoughts about how this can affect the way individuals view themselves.

Independent Practice: The instructor along with students will create a list of activities that can boost self-perception on flip chart paper. The list will include: create an affirmation, set a small goal you know you can achieve, do a good deed for someone, practice self-care (haircut, new hairstyle, work out, wear your favorite outfit, or meditate), remove "I can't" from your vocabulary to adopt a Growth Mindset, stop comparing yourself to others and understand that you are enough, learn how to congratulate yourself, and be patient with your progress. Students will choose two activities to further expand on. Students will predict and document the positive effects of engaging in the chosen activities.

Lesson Wrap Up: Students will answer why is having an accurate self-perception important? Students will document responses in their workbook.

*Challenge: Identify lyrics in a song that you like that displays a healthy relationship, the lyrics must be clean!

MOUNT CLEMENS, MI

We now head 20 miles Northeast of Detroit to the former rose capital of the United States, Mount Clemens, Michigan. "Can't be afraid of heights up where we sit"[7] is where this lyrical breakdown begins! When I heard that lyric I internalized and used it to build up my self-confidence, and now I offer it up to you to boost yours. As I repeat the line again think deeply about what is being said. You cannot be afraid of heights up where we sit! I hear that and I think to myself what number is at the top of any list... #1. When a person feels that they are on top of their game you can tell in their demeanor, their swagger, and they possess the type of confidence that a winner has. You also have a different kind of focus towards the things you want to accomplish. You do not engage with things like most people because you know it takes extra to become extraordinary. They do not call it Mamba Mentality for no reason (KOBE!).

YOU HAVE GREATNESS INSIDE OF YOU, but you typically see this type of confidence in people when it comes to sports or their hobbies where they have achieved mastery. I'm pushing for this same mentality both on and off the playing field. That same feeling you get when you make a shot, score a goal, take a really good selfie, beat a video game, create a nice caption on Instagram, or do a dance challenge on TikTok should be the same feeling you get when you do well on an assignment or test at school, have a productive shift, or complete a project at work. We are working out the SELF-AWARENESS muscles here. Our mindset is so powerful in how we interact in this world. Your thoughts drive your actions (MESSAGE!). If you do not think highly of yourself then your actions will be of the self-destructive type, and you will sabotage your own progress thinking that success is not your rightful place. I cannot allow that kind of thinking to continue. You got this! You have all the necessary tools you need inside of you. You can be an excellent athlete, the best dressed person, be respected by your peers, and STILL be a great student. Do not be afraid of the heights you can reach, apply that same energy to every part of your life.

LESSON PLAN FOR MOUNT CLEMENS

Materials Needed: Flip chart paper, markers, pens or pencils, and student's workbooks.

Objective: Students will train their SELF-AWARENESS muscles by challenging negative self-talk and thoughts. (**Skill – SELF-EFFICACY**)

CCSS.ELA: RL.9-10.1 Cite strong and thorough textual evidence to support analysis of what the text says explicitly as well as inferences drawn from the text. RL.9-10.2 Determine a theme of a text and analyze in detail its development over the course of the text, including how it emerges and is shaped and refined by specific details; provide an objective summary of the text. W.9-10.2 Write informative/explanatory texts to examine and convey complex ideas, concepts, and information clearly and accurately through the effective selection, organization, and analysis of content. SL.9-10.1 Initiate and participate effectively in a range of collaborative discussions (one-on-one, in groups, and teacher-led) with diverse partners on grades 9–10 topics, texts, and issues, building on others' ideas and expressing their own clearly and persuasively.

Appetizer: What is the theme of this text?

Vocabulary: The instructor will review the vocabulary words. The instructor will ask for examples of each vocabulary word. Demeanor- Outward behavior or bearing. Extraordinary- Going beyond what is usual, regular, or customary. Mastery- Possession or display of great skill or technique. Self-Efficacy- An individual's confidence in their ability to complete a task or achieve a goal.

Prior Knowledge- The instructor will ask each student what they are really good at and then ask how did they become that good at it?

New Knowledge- The instructor will encourage students to stop saying that they cannot do something. The instructor will encourage students to change their mindset to they have not mastered it yet. The instructor will question students on how they can apply the same focus of the things they do well on to the things they need to improve upon.

Guided Practice: If You Can Believe It, You Can Achieve It. The instructor along with students will document the four key themes of Self-Efficacy on flip chart paper. The instructor will place these four words on the top of the paper: Personal Experience, Social Modeling, Social Persuasion, and Emotion. Under Personal Experience the instructor will write, you feel more confident about a task when you have successfully done it multiple times. Under Social Modeling the instructor will write, when you see others successfully complete a task it boosts your belief that you can complete it. Under Social Persuasion the instructor will write, if someone tells you that they think you will do well on a task, it increases your belief that you can. Under Emotion the instructor will write how you feel determines your confidence level for completing a task.

Independent Practice: Students will take a subject that they feel they do poorly in and apply the four key themes of Self-Efficacy to boost their confidence in that subject. Students will define and explain how they can use Personal Experience, Social Modeling, Social Persuasion, and Emotion to increase their confidence. Students will write an explanatory text to present to the class.

Lesson Wrap Up: Students will form a sequential restorative circle, the instructor will ask what are the four key themes of Self-Efficacy?

*Challenge: Identify lyrics in a song that you like that talk about being confident in your abilities, the lyrics must be clean!

Lagos, NIGERIA

We will need to get our virtual passport stamped as we travel to Africa! This analysis is a perfect example of how being socially aware of another person's culture can benefit you and it can extend beyond an educational situation. When you have finely tuned your SOCIAL AWARENESS muscles your RELATIONSHIP SKILL muscles grow too, and you find it easier to interact with all types of people. This breakdown is not about a lyric, it is more about knowledge about a specific artist, and in this situation it involves a Nigerian rapper. My knowledge of his musical catalog served me in building a relationship with an elementary student.

Let me explain, staff were having issues with a student at a school I was supporting where the student was new to the United States. The staff could not tell me where this young man was from, all they could tell me about were the issues they were having with him. When I got a chance to talk to that student the first question I asked him should have been asked long before I even came to that school. I asked what country he was from. With hesitation he responded Nigeria and then asked did I know where that was? I responded yes, and when I told him that I was born in the United Kingdom and specifically London he visibly became more relaxed. I explained to him that I grew up in a few different countries myself and I know all about the Naija people, and his standoffish demeanor gave way to a smile. I then asked him if he listened to Wizkid and an excited YES came blurting out! I played the track "Ojuelegba" for him as we recited the lyrics.

Long story short, I was able to connect with that young man and helped him to understand the expectations of the school. That connection would have not been possible if I did not know about his culture. Never forget that **YOU HAVE GREATNESS INSIDE OF YOU!** Take time to immerse yourself into different cultures and languages. Venture out of your comfort zone by listening to music from different countries, attending cultural festivals or parades, and seeking friendships with diverse individuals. This will create opportunities to connect and in those moments when people make the assumption that you are not cultured, you can defeat those misconceptions and your **GREATNESS** will shine through!

LESSON PLAN FOR LAGOS

Materials Needed: Pens, markers or pencils, student's workbooks, and computers with internet access.

Objective: Students will train their SOCIAL AWARENESS muscles by creating a presentation for a country outside of the United States. (**Skill – APPRECIATING DIVERSITY**)

CCSS.ELA: RL.9-10.1 Cite strong and thorough textual evidence to support analysis of what the text says explicitly as well as inferences drawn from the text. RL.9-10.2 Determine a theme of a text and analyze in detail its development over the course of the text, including how it emerges and is shaped and refined by specific details; provide an objective summary of the text. W.9-10.7 Conduct short as well as more sustained research projects to answer a question (including a self-generated question) or solve a problem; narrow or broaden the inquiry when appropriate; synthesize multiple sources on the subject, demonstrating understanding of the subject under investigation. SL.9-10.1 Initiate and participate effectively in a range of collaborative discussions (one-on-one, in groups, and teacher-led) with diverse partners on grades 9–10 topics, texts, and issues, building on others' ideas and expressing their own clearly and persuasively. SL.9-10.5 Make strategic use of digital media in presentations to enhance understanding of findings, reasoning, and evidence and to add interest.

Appetizer: What is the theme of this text?

Vocabulary: The instructor will review the vocabulary words. The instructor will ask for examples of each vocabulary word. Culture- The customs, arts, social institutions, and achievements of a particular nation, people, or other social group. Diverse- Including many different types of people or things. Misconception- a view or opinion that is incorrect based on faulty thinking or understanding. Naija- A nickname for people from the country of Nigeria.

Prior Knowledge- The instructor will ask students if they know any information about a culture/country outside of their own.

38

New Knowledge- The instructor will explain that people often have misconceptions about people who come from different countries to the United States. The instructor will inform students that misconceptions can play a huge factor on how people view those cultures. The instructor will state that every country has their own unique culture and appreciating another's culture helps to build relationships.

Guided Practice: The instructor along with the students will gather information about the country of Nigeria. The instructor along with the students will create a power point presentation. The instructor and students will search for: languages spoken, currency, when it became an independent country, notable people, capital city, music, picture of the flag, which continent it is a part of, and a popular food dish. Videos documenting the culture can also be added to the presentation.

Independent Practice: Students will choose one country from The Caribbean Islands, South America, Africa, Europe, or Asia to repeat the activity from the guided practice. Students will create a power point presentation. Students will present the information to the class.

Lesson Wrap Up: Students will answer what was the most interesting thing they learned about their country. Students will document responses in their workbook.

*Challenge: Find a music artist from the country you reported on, share their name and type of music they perform.

Harlem, NY

As we return back to the United States we land in the place where Langston Hughes made his name during the 1920's cultural Renaissance for African Americans! Let me welcome you to Harlem and the lyric "The meaning of the name David is beloved or friend"[8] is extremely important to me! We are exercising our SELF-AWARENESS muscles as we dive into this lyrical analysis. Typically when a person speaks the phrase you need to live up to your name, it is in a negative way because it implies that the individual is not meeting an expectation. Most people take it as not doing anything that will embarrass the family name which is usually the last name. What about an individual's first name? It has probably never crossed your mind to find out if your first name has any significance. I knew I was named after my father but upon hearing that lyric at age 31 it gave my first name new meaning and guided me towards the energy that I intentionally try to give off.

That opening line states that the name David means beloved or friend. The definition of beloved is a much-loved person and we all know a friend is a person with whom you share a mutual bond of affection outside of a significant other or family member. This was a whole new level of SELF-AWARENESS for me. I have always been about sending out positive energy to the world to help others, and there is a direct correlation between the meaning of my name and the way I carry myself. I take pride in knowing one of the meanings of my first name. This is important to remember when I find myself in a bad situation or in those down times. I can revert back to the meaning of my name to boost my emotional state. I keep telling you all that **YOU HAVE GREATNESS INSIDE OF YOU!** You may not already have lyrics that have highlighted your name like this track has for me, but you now have the opportunity to connect your name with something that has value to you. You get to use your creativity to Big Up yourself by combining your strengths into your name!

LESSON PLAN FOR HARLEM

Materials Needed: Pens or pencils, student's workbooks, computers with internet and printer access.

Objective: Students will train their SELF-AWARENESS muscles by taking the VIA Character Strengths survey and creating a Word Art image based on their name, character strengths, and hobbies. (SKILL – RECOGNIZING STRENGTHS)

CCSS.ELA: RL.9-10.2 Determine a theme of a text and analyze in detail its development over the course of the text, including how it emerges and is shaped and refined by specific details; provide an objective summary of the text. W.9-10.3 Write narratives to develop real or imagined experiences or events using effective technique, well-chosen details, and well-structured event sequences. W.9-10.6 Use technology, including the Internet, to produce, publish, and update individual or shared writing products, taking advantage of technology's capacity to link to other information and to display information flexibly and dynamically. SL.9-10.1 Initiate and participate effectively in a range of collaborative discussions (one-on-one, in groups, and teacher-led) with diverse partners on grades 9–10 topics, texts, and issues, building on others' ideas and expressing their own clearly and persuasively.

Appetizer: What is the theme of this text?

Vocabulary: The instructor will review the vocabulary words. The instructor will ask for examples of each vocabulary word. Big Up- An expression of support and encouragement, to praise. Creativity- Having the quality or power to create meaningful new ideas. Strength- A strong attribute or inherent asset.

Prior Knowledge- The instructor will ask students if anyone knows the meaning of their first name or if it has a special meaning in a different culture? The instructor will ask students if they believe power can come from a name.

Guided Practice: VIA Character Strengths survey. The instructor along with the students will log onto viacharacter.org and click on "Take the free survey". There are two options, one for adults and one for students. The instructor should complete a survey while the students are completing theirs. All participants will need to enter an email address. The instructor will assist students who need help understanding words and context. Once the surveys are complete the instructor along with the students can share their results with the class, print out the results. The instructor will print out a copy of each student's strengths to keep at school. The instructor will ask if students agree with their strength profile and how they show their top strength.

Independent Practice: Word Art Activity. Students will log onto wordart.com and click the "create now" button. Students will type in their first name, the top five (5) of their character strengths, a nickname (if applicable), and five (5) things they like about themselves or their hobbies. Students will then customize the shape, font, layout, and style for their word art. Students will present their word art to the class and tell the class why they chose they shape they did.

Lesson Wrap Up: Students will answer what are some new strengths they learned about themselves? How can they incorporate their new strengths into everyday life? Students will document responses in their workbook.

*Challenge: Identify lyrics in a song that you like that makes you feel good about yourself, the lyrics must be clean!

Fayetteville, NC

The lyrics I have been presenting to you are all personal to me, but this lyric is even more personal because it speaks to an insecurity of mine that I dealt with growing up. When the artist raps, "I keep my twisted grill, just to show the kids it's real"[9] is powerful to a person whose teeth are not perfect either. It is also a boost of confidence to all to see a big star going through something that a lot of people can connect with. Just like the artist here, my teeth not being "perfect" never stopped me from being successful. YOU HAVE GREATNESS INSIDE OF YOU! It does not matter if you have a crooked smile or not! Most people are insecure about something, but you cannot allow that to stop your GREATNESS.

This track is working out our SELF-AWARENESS muscles. When you can identify your emotions you are able to create an accurate self-perception, and it gives you a starting place for growth. Your strength (inner strength), effort and persistence, optimism, and confidence towards reaching success is not dependent upon your physical appearance, height, weight, or clothes you wear. Focus on building your character traits, and know that your self-worth should not be based on superficial things or expectations from social media. This track drops so many gems about being comfortable in your own skin, being proud, and confident within yourself! Do not put too much stock into the negative things that people will say to and about you. We all need to exercise the practice of giving our mental energy to the people who care about us and stop giving it to the ones who do not. It has been mentioned before in this book, but I will say it again, you are your own movement!

LESSON PLAN FOR FAYETTEVILLE

Materials Needed: Pens, markers or pencils, and student's workbooks.

Objective: Students will train their SELF-AWARENESS muscles by continuing to evaluate the results of their VIA Character Strengths survey. (**Skill – RECOGNIZING STRENGTHS**)

CCSS.ELA: RL.9-10.1 Cite strong and thorough textual evidence to support analysis of what the text says explicitly as well as inferences drawn from the text. RL.9-10.2 Determine a theme of a text and analyze in detail its development over the course of the text, including how it emerges and is shaped and refined by specific details; provide an objective summary of the text. W.9-10.3 Write narratives to develop real or imagined experiences or events using effective technique, well-chosen details, and well-structured event sequences. SL.9-10.1 Initiate and participate effectively in a range of collaborative discussions (one-on-one, in groups, and teacher-led) with diverse partners on grades 9–10 topics, texts, and issues, building on others' ideas and expressing their own clearly and persuasively.

Appetizer: What is the theme of this text?

Vocabulary: The instructor will review the vocabulary words. The instructor will ask for examples of each vocabulary word. Character- the mental and moral qualities distinctive to an individual. Dropping Gems- Sharing useful knowledge or information. Insecurity- Uncertainty or anxiety about oneself. Superficial- Existing or occurring at or on the surface.

Prior Knowledge- The instructor will ask students what are some expectations from social media that find themselves believing in. The instructor will ask students how they feel about themselves if they do not measure up to those expectations.

New Knowledge- The instructor will encourage students that if they cannot change something about themselves they really should embrace it!

46

Guided Practice: What it look like. The instructor along will ask students to write down some things they want to improve on. The instructor will inform the class that this is a safe space and we will be building each other up during this activity. The instructor will model for the students when someone states their one thing the entire class will respond "You got this! You look like greatness to me!" The activity will end after every student gets praised by the class.

Independent Practice: Story time. The instructor will hand out each student's print out of their list of 24 character strengths. The students will focus on strengths six through ten (6-10) for this activity. Each student will write down and share how they display each character strength. For example: The instructor's sixth strength is kindness, they will create a story about a time where they helped someone find their dog. The class will respond "Look like greatness to me!" after each student shares their one strength and short story that accompanies it with the class.

Lesson Wrap Up: Students will assess the importance of inner strength. Students will document responses in their workbook.

*Challenge: Identify lyrics in a song that you like that talks about inner strength, the lyrics must be clean!

Brevoort Houses, BED-STUY

We are heading back to Brooklyn for this lyrical breakdown, but many people may ask why I would include the following lyric in a book that was created to motivate, inspire growth, and help people succeed. "My daddy left me, and he ain't even die"[10] is a constant reminder of the many students I have interacted with over the years whose reality is that lyric. The ways this type of situation can manifest for a young person can be very detrimental to their self-perception, ability to trust, and affect many parts of their life negatively. It can even affect them as an adult if they have never dealt with those emotions (MESSAGE!). The message I want to convey is clear, even though a bad situation occurred you can still grow to be an amazing individual. This type of situation can strengthen your SELF-AWARENESS muscles with an emphasis on identifying emotions and being resilient. Another muscle group being worked are your RELATIONSHIP SKILLS. You do not have to hide negative emotions, we all experience them and addressing them can be difficult but that is where our strength lies.

I have heard the wise person say, I guess knowing I'm weak is when I'm really being strong. I am not saying weak in a derogatory sense towards physical or mental strength. I am speaking facts about us being human and at times we will feel down, and we will be affected by things that have happened to us. Getting help from people in your circle is fine but there is no shame in talking to a professional either. If your doctor told you that you have Cancer and gave you the plan for treatment, would you ignore them and continue going on about your life? No, you would follow the plan and fight to get better! For many people the task appears too strenuous to move forward from traumatic experiences. They often carry that baggage throughout life, but stress like a deadly disease can kill you. You can progress, never forget that YOU HAVE GREATNESS INSIDE OF YOU! That greatness does not disappear when things are bad, like I told you in the introduction it is there from the day you are born. Even if this situation does not apply to you, work on being empathetic to others because you can be their source of strength. You can overcome anything you undergo with the right mindset and surrounding yourself with the right people (MESSAGE!).

LESSON PLAN FOR BREVOORT HOUSES

Materials Needed: Play-Doh or clay, pens, markers or pencils, and student's workbooks.

Objective: Students will train their SELF-AWARENESS muscles by participating in a hands on activity that will highlight their resiliency. Students will train their SOCIAL AWARENESS muscles by creating scenarios where they assisted someone going through a tough time. (**SKILLS – ACCURATE SELF-PERCEPTION AND EMPATHY**)

CCSS.ELA: RL.9-10.1 Cite strong and thorough textual evidence to support analysis of what the text says explicitly as well as inferences drawn from the text. RL.9-10.2 Determine a theme of a text and analyze in detail its development over the course of the text, including how it emerges and is shaped and refined by specific details; provide an objective summary of the text. W.9-10.3 Write narratives to develop real or imagined experiences or events using effective technique, well-chosen details, and well-structured event sequences. SL.9-10.1 Initiate and participate effectively in a range of collaborative discussions (one-on-one, in groups, and teacher-led) with diverse partners on grades 9–10 topics, texts, and issues, building on others' ideas and expressing their own clearly and persuasively.

Appetizer: What is the theme of this text?

Vocabulary: The instructor will review the vocabulary words. The instructor will ask for examples of each vocabulary word. Detrimental- Tending to cause harm. Empathy- The ability to understand and share the feelings of another. Resilient- Able to withstand or recover quickly from difficult conditions. Strenuous- Requiring or using great exertion.

Prior Knowledge- The instructor will ask students if they know someone that comes from a single parent or two parent household, stays with their grandparent or another family member, stays in a group home, stays in a hotel, stays in the suburbs, stays in a nice house, or shelter. The instructor will ask students can people still reach greatness regardless of their situation. Why or why not?

New Knowledge- This will serve as a mini activity. The instructor will ask students to close their eyes and think about a bad moment in their lives for 10 seconds (use the stopwatch on your phone).The instructor will tell the students to open their eyes, take a deep breath, and remind them that they made it through that bad moment. The instructor will have the students clap for themselves and state that they can move forward to their greatness.

Guided Practice: Build me up! The instructor will give every student a can of Play-Doh or clay (whatever is available) and encourage them to try to build something.   After 2-3 minutes, the instructor will tell the students to smash/pound/rip apart their creation. The instructor will explain to students that this is them when a bad situation occurs. The instructor will have the students create a ball out their Play-Doh and recreate their first creation. The instructor will re-state the definition of resilient and explain to the students that they like the Play-Doh are able to come back to form. The instructor will remind students that they have recovered from difficult situations already and they have to keep going towards greatness.

Independent Practice: Build you up! The instructor will prompt students to create a scenario where they are being a source of strength for someone going through a bad situation. The student will document the event that took place, how they assisted the person, and what other resources/people could they have offered to help with the situation?

Lesson Wrap Up: Students will form a sequential restorative circle and the instructor will create a chant describing resilience. Possible examples: keep on pushing, we are warriors, or if you fall down get right back up.

*__Challenge__: Identify lyrics in a song that you like that talk about overcoming a bad situation, the lyrics must be clean!

ATLANTA, GA

Our next destination was known as the mecca for the Civil Rights Movement in the 1960s, let's ride down I-95 as we enter Atlanta, Georgia. This lyric offers a truth that all successful people know, "When you working hard then your money start expanding."[11] For the youth, I want you to think about expanding opportunities. Focus on loving the process, and if you do that money will naturally come from your efforts. I envision a motivational speaker quoting that line and then highlighting the natural process of plant, cultivate, and then harvest. All my farmers know but let me break it down for everyone else, the day you plant the seed is not the day you eat the fruit! People of the world, not everything can be acquired with an instant gratification mindset. There is no Uber Eats or DoorDash that will bring success to your front door! Let me remind everyone reading this book that an important piece to living your best life is your mindset. Anything you want in life you must put the work in. The question of the day then becomes how bad do you want success? Success is yours to own because **YOU HAVE GREATNESS INSIDE OF YOU!**

I am speaking to an individual's SELF-MANAGEMENT muscles on this one. You must be disciplined and intrinsically motivated to keep pushing even when you do not get the results right away. If you look at successful people in any area of life you learn that countless hours went into working on their craft, and they did not become the best at what they did after a few times of trying (**MESSAGE!**). Most importantly, they did not stop until they conquered the goal (**MESSAGE!**). There is no such thing as an overnight success story. Would you be willing to dedicate yourself to a goal knowing it would take 10 years before you reap the harvest? Let me give you some advice for when times do get tough, do not complain, it does not make the situation any better or easier! Those who are working hard stand out from the crowd due to that simple fact, they are working hard. There is an article on primermagazine.com entitled "Hard Work in 5 Easy Steps: Understanding Perseverance in The Modern Age" (Busch, 2012) and there is one line that perfectly sums up the message of this lyrical breakdown, "Hard work is above and beyond and it's the **ONLY** thing that will push you above and beyond!"

LESSON PLAN FOR ATLANTA

Materials Needed: Flip chart paper, markers or pencils, and student's workbooks.

Objective: Students will train their SELF-MANAGEMENT muscles by regulating their thoughts and discovering their "why". (**Skill – SELF-MOTIVATION**)

CCSS.ELA: RL.9-10.1 Cite strong and thorough textual evidence to support analysis of what the text says explicitly as well as inferences drawn from the text. RL.9-10.2 Determine a theme of a text and analyze in detail its development over the course of the text, including how it emerges and is shaped and refined by specific details; provide an objective summary of the text. W.9-10.3 Write narratives to develop real or imagined experiences or events using effective technique, well-chosen details, and well-structured event sequences. SL.9-10.1 Initiate and participate effectively in a range of collaborative discussions (one-on-one, in groups, and teacher-led) with diverse partners on grades 9–10 topics, texts, and issues, building on others' ideas and expressing their own clearly and persuasively.

Appetizer: What is the theme of this text?

Vocabulary: The instructor will review the vocabulary words. The instructor will ask for examples of each vocabulary word. Instant Gratification- Immediate satisfaction, reward at once. Mindset- A mental attitude or inclination. Mecca- A place regarded as a center for a specified group, activity, or interest. Perseverance- Continued effort to do or achieve something despite difficulties, failure, or opposition. Self-Motivation- Driven by one's own desires and ambitions.

Prior Knowledge- The instructor will ask students if they like Thanksgiving dinner. The instructor will then ask students which meal they would enjoy more, Thanksgiving dinner or getting food from a drive thru. The instructor will compare the time it takes to prepare a Thanksgiving spread and the quality of the food. The instructor will explain to the students that the same thing can be said for the amount of time they dedicate to their goals. There is a correlation between the time spent working towards a goal and actually achieving the goal.

New Knowledge- The instructor will state to students that achieving their goals is just like a car, they both need fuel to get from the starting point to the final destination. The instructor will communicate that their why is the fuel to their goals. The instructor will explain to students that their why needs to be something personal to them and strong enough to keep them going when they are tired, things aren't going right, the weather is bad, etc. The instructor will state to students that their why should not be focused on money because when there is no longer that incentive they will lose motivation. The instructor will remind students that their why is important because as mentioned earlier, success does not happen overnight so how will they stay motivated? It's their why.

Guided Practice: Find your Why, part 1. The instructor along with students will determine the potential "why" for graduating high school. The instructor will write High School Graduation in the middle of flip chart paper. Students along with the instructor will work together to select meaningful reasons for an individual to stay motivated to graduate.

Independent Practice: Find your Why, part 2. Students will choose one academic and personal goal from their vision board and determine the "whys" that will keep them motivated until they complete their goals. If one of their goals was to graduate high school then students must choose another goal.

Lesson Wrap Up: Students will form a sequential restorative circle, and the instructor will ask why is their "why" important towards achieving a goal?

*Challenge: Identify lyrics in a song that you like that talk about not quitting, the lyrics must be clean!

TORONTO, CANADA

YOU HAVE GREATNESS INSIDE OF YOU and this lyric drives home that message as we land in Toronto, the capital city of the province of Ontario. "I'm treating every year like it's game seven"[12] is the point of emphasis for this lyrical breakdown, and we are working out our SELF-MANAGEMENT muscles. In sports, game seven is the deciding game or match in a best of seven series. Which means if you lose game seven then your season is over! Game seven is where you forget about all your previous mistakes and shortcomings of the past few games because, this is the finale. You want to bring your best to advance to the next round or to win the championship. I want to take it even further for anyone reading this book. What if we treated EVERYDAY like it was game seven?

I am speaking to the fact that life will not end the next day but what if we forgot about the errors of the past and focus our energy on giving our best today! The failures of yesterday will not hinder me from progressing today. You create the narrative for your story. You will make mistakes along the way but how will you rise back from them? We all can benefit from having a short-term memory when it comes to our failures. If we can adopt this mindset EVERYDAY, we are being consistent towards creating positive habits. Be mindful that the things you do the most become your habits and they can be either positive or negative! I will let you all decide on which habits help you towards achieving a goal, and sorry procrastination is not welcome here as it only takes you further from your goals.

More importantly, you cannot reach a goal if you have not set out one to achieve. This goes back to your mindset, channeling your thoughts towards achieving a goal. You have already created a whole vision board filled with your goals! There is no excuse to not be working towards an academic or personal goal. No matter how big or small the goal is, once you achieve it your confidence grows. I encourage you all to be an active participant in life. We must stop coasting through life and just going through the motions. Never think that you cannot be great, just go out there and be great. Success is determined by the race you are running against yourself not others (MESSAGE!), being better than who you were yesterday.

LESSON PLAN FOR TORONTO

Materials Needed: Flip chart paper, markers, pens or pencils, and student's workbooks.

Objective: Students will train their SELF-MANAGEMENT muscles by integrating the game seven concept to increase their productivity. (**Skill – SELF-MOTIVATION**)

CCSS.ELA: RL.9-10.1 Cite strong and thorough textual evidence to support analysis of what the text says explicitly as well as inferences drawn from the text. RL.9-10.2 Determine a theme of a text and analyze in detail its development over the course of the text, including how it emerges and is shaped and refined by specific details; provide an objective summary of the text. W.9-10.3 Write narratives to develop real or imagined experiences or events using effective technique, well-chosen details, and well-structured event sequences. SL.9-10.1 Initiate and participate effectively in a range of collaborative discussions (one-on-one, in groups, and teacher-led) with diverse partners on grades 9–10 topics, texts, and issues, building on others' ideas and expressing their own clearly and persuasively.

Appetizer: What is the theme of this text?

Vocabulary: The instructor will review the vocabulary words. The instructor will ask for examples of each vocabulary word. Consistent- Acting or done in the same way over time. Habit- A behavior pattern acquired by frequent repetition. Procrastination- Delay or postpone action, put off doing something. Productivity- The state or quality of producing something.

Prior Knowledge- The instructor will ask students if they have ever made the statement "I'll just do it tomorrow." The instructor will then ask students how often they actually complete the task or does it get put off again.

New Knowledge- The instructor will encourage students that moving forward every day is game seven and they are either being consistent or procrastinating towards achieving their goals.

Guided Practice: The instructor along with students will create a list of strategies to decrease procrastination on flip chart paper. The instructor will write: choosing a specific time to study, finding mini-motivators to reward themselves, and eliminating distractions (cell phone, television, being in a loud room) to increase focus. The students will then join in to generate more strategies to decrease procrastination.

Independent Practice: Every day is game seven. Students will update their academic goal (if needed) and write down new action steps towards achieving the goal with the focus of everyday being the championship game. Students will incorporate some strategies to decrease their procrastination. For students who have achieved their academic goal, the plan will be created for the personal goal they chose during the first session.

Lesson Wrap Up: Students will take the phase, the things you do the most become your habits. Students will reflect on if their habits are positive or negative. Students will create a narrative outlining the activities they spend the most time doing, if it benefits an academic or personal goal of theirs, and is there evidence to change to an activity to a more productive one. Students can defend their activity but will have to show its benefit towards completing a goal. Students will document responses in their workbook.

*__Challenge__: Identify lyrics in a song that you like that talk about achieving goals, the lyrics must be clean!

CHICAGO, IL

This lyric has been challenging me since my senior year of high school. "We got arms, but won't reach for the skies"[13] hits me like an 18-wheeler because the statement is so true. Benjamin Disraeli stated, "Action may not always bring happiness; but there is no happiness without action." Yes, we are working out our SELF-AWARENESS muscles. This lyric also reminds me of a former client I had when I worked in mental health. This client asked me why I did this job, at the time I was a Qualified Professional working on an Intensive In-Home Counseling team. When I asked him to explain what he meant he responded that helping people was not a black man's job and how come I did not become a barber or a mechanic. I then asked him if those were the best jobs black men can have? Which he answered no, probably a rapper or an athlete. This lyric came flooding into my mind with the quickness. I am here to tell anybody black, white, brown, yellow, green on this Earth that you can achieve any goal you want to, why? YOU HAVE GREATNESS INSIDE OF YOU!

That conversation was one of the realist I have had with a client. He did not believe that he could be greater than the status quo, and his environment had led him to believe that his ceiling was only that of an athlete or rapper. He did not have the self-confidence to go his own way due to what the culture thinks he should be based on biases. There were many times where I reminded him that he does not have to follow that mold. You have the power to change your current situation and be whatever you want but it will take being uncomfortable to make it happen. Like the quote states, "if nothing changes, then nothing will change." You cannot experience success if you are only doing the things that have led you to failure. My client had me to pour positive energy into him which is helpful but the change must come from within, an inside-out approach. Embrace being dedicated to your goals if you want to change. Understand this, the road to success will put you on a different path. This new path will require you to break away from the people who are just following the trends and not their vision of what they could be.

LESSON PLAN FOR CHICAGO

Materials Needed: Lined or copier paper, pens, markers or pencils, and student's workbooks.

Objective: Students will train their SELF-AWARENESS muscles by engaging in an activity designed to boost their optimism. Students will also train their RELATIONSHIP SKILL muscles by creating a mentor contract. (**Skills – SELF-CONFIDENCE AND RELATIONSHIP BUILDING**)

CCSS.ELA: RL.9-10.2 Determine a theme of a text and analyze in detail its development over the course of the text, including how it emerges and is shaped and refined by specific details; provide an objective summary of the text. W.9-10.3 Write narratives to develop real or imagined experiences or events using effective technique, well-chosen details, and well-structured event sequences. SL.9-10.1 Initiate and participate effectively in a range of collaborative discussions (one-on-one, in groups, and teacher-led) with diverse partners on grades 9–10 topics, texts, and issues, building on others' ideas and expressing their own clearly and persuasively.

Appetizer: What is the theme of this text?

Vocabulary: The instructor will review the vocabulary words. The instructor will ask for examples of each vocabulary word. Manifest- To show something clearly, through signs or actions. Mentor- A person who gives a younger or inexperienced person help and advice over a period of time. Self-Confidence- A feeling of trust in one's abilities, qualities, and judgment. Status Quo- The existing state of affairs, especially regarding social issues.

Prior Knowledge- The instructor will ask students if they think every successful person truly did it on their own without the support of anybody. The instructor will then ask students if they think having positive people assisting them will increase their chance of success.

New Knowledge- The instructor will state that having self-confidence and getting guidance from a mentor are major parts of the recipe for success of any type. The instructor will encourage students to take the mindset of a sponge, and soak up knowledge and information from different sources.

Guided Practice: Paper Ball Activity. The instructor will hand students a blank piece of paper, have them write their names at the top and ask them if anyone has ever told them that they could not accomplish something. The instructor will ask students to write down one (1) to five (5) things someone told them they could not do or something they believe they cannot do. The instructor will then retrieve a clean trash can and have students line up a few feet away. The instructor will explain that thinking you cannot achieve something is trash and ask them to ball up their paper and shoot it in the trash can, one at a time. Every student will shoot their paper ball in the trash can. The instructor will have students go get their ball out of the trashcan. The instructor will ask the student if they still feel they cannot achieve those things. If the student responds yes, they will take their paper ball and line back up until every student responds. Repeat a few times and encourage the student that they can achieve the goal, the idea that they cannot is trash.

Independent Practice: Mentor Me Please. Students will create a personalized mentor contract. The template will have the definition of mentor on it, a space for the student's name, and a space for the potential mentor. The language will state by signing this mentor contract you acknowledge to assist the student during this school year. The students will determine the activities they will engage in with their mentor. Some examples: meeting parent/guardian, a formal face to face meeting weekly for 15 minutes, daily morning affirmation meetings, attending at least three (3) extracurricular activities (if the student plays sports or is in a club), monthly evaluation of their vision board goals, and assist with issues with another teacher. Students must pick four activities to assign their mentor to. Students will bring back the signed form during the next session.

Lesson Wrap Up: Students will answer what is one profession they feel they cannot be involved in due to their: race, perceived intelligence, neighborhood, etc. Students will deconstruct those negative statements and document how they can overcome to be successful in the profession they chose. Students will document responses in their workbook.

***Challenge**: Ask your mentor to attend the next session!

WESTON ROAD, TORONTO

We are going back to Toronto as we have reached our last stop on this journey of Social Emotional Learning lessons we can obtain from Hip-Hop. I hope through this journey you have learned that Social Emotional Learning is vital to the success of a person, now let's finish strong! This lesson should motivate everyone across the nation and world when it comes to senseless acts of violence. This lyrical analysis focuses on our RELATIONSHIP SKILLS, SOCIAL AWARENESS, and RESPONSIBLE DECISION-MAKING muscles. The lyric is "What is the point of all the beefing when we really blood?"[14] You can look at the line in many ways but I feel it is speaking to my culture and why we constantly tear each other down when we can easily move forward together. Another way you could look at it is even though you have an issue with someone it does not have to result in violence. When I heard the lyric, I thought about the state of our society but mostly the youth. They are always ready to talk negatively, troll, fight or cause harm to the ones that look like them when there is a conflict. Why at the first sign of perceived disrespect do they seem to exhaust every resource just to get revenge? I continue to lose students and friends to beef because we do not empower people to build these Social Emotional muscles.

I am speaking to the youth when I say if you used that same energy towards schoolwork, your goals, and things that matter you would be unstoppable (MESSAGE!). Too many times a decision gets made in anger and choices made in anger cannot be undone. Let's all say it together, YOU HAVE GREATNESS INSIDE OF YOU! These are skills that I still strive to be better at: communication and problem solving for the betterment of everyone in a situation. Also, weighing out the consequences of an action before I do them. There is strength in knowing when to seek assistance whether it is bringing in an administrator in a school conflict, a supervisor in a dispute with a coworker, or a moderator in any type of conflict. Avoiding unnecessary conflict does not make you a punk (MESSAGE!). Conflict can happen from early childhood to adulthood so gaining these skills will benefit you for a lifetime. Understanding that a level of respect must be attained even if you are not "friends" with an individual is important. You will not like or be liked by everyone you interact with and that is ok. Do not allow that to stop your progress and get you out of your character.

LESSON PLAN FOR WESTON ROAD

Materials Needed: Pens or pencils, student's workbooks, and computers with internet access.

Objective: Students will train their RESPONSIBLE DECISION-MAKING muscles by evaluating the realistic consequences of various actions. (SKILLS – ANALYZING SITUATIONS AND SOLVING PROBLEMS)

CCSS.ELA: RL.9-10.1 Cite strong and thorough textual evidence to support analysis of what the text says explicitly as well as inferences drawn from the text. RL.9-10.2 Determine a theme of a text and analyze in detail its development over the course of the text, including how it emerges and is shaped and refined by specific details; provide an objective summary of the text. W.9-10.3 Write narratives to develop real or imagined experiences or events using effective technique, well-chosen details, and well-structured event sequences. SL.9-10.1 Initiate and participate effectively in a range of collaborative discussions (one-on-one, in groups, and teacher-led) with diverse partners on grades 9–10 topics, texts, and issues, building on others' ideas and expressing their own clearly and persuasively. SL.9-10.3 Evaluate a speaker's point of view, reasoning, and use of evidence and rhetoric, identifying any fallacious reasoning or exaggerated or distorted evidence.

Appetizer: What is the theme of this text?

Vocabulary: The instructor will review the vocabulary words. The instructor will ask for examples of each vocabulary word. Beef- An ongoing problem between two people or two groups of people. Retaliate- Make an attack or assault in return of a similar attack. Troll- To harass, criticize, or antagonize someone by making disparaging public statements, postings, or acts.

Prior Knowledge- The instructor will state the quote "An eye for an eye only ends up making the whole world blind". The instructor will question students about the meaning of the quote. The instructor will then ask the students if they feel when someone does something to them, they have to do something back. Why is that the norm?

Guided Practice: The instructor will quote Stephen Covey by stating "We are free to choose our actions, but we are not free to choose the consequences of those actions." The instructor will use the analogy of when you pick up one end of the stick you pick up the other. Students will cut out their consequences flash card from page 49-51. The first activity students will use the cards with FIGHT as the action. Students will pair up, and take turns evaluating the consequences for their actions. The next activity students will use the cards with STUDY, CYBER BULLY, and BE NICE, but this time they will create their own consequences for the action. During the last activity students will create both the actions and the consequences. The instructor will remind the students that they indeed choose their action but do not get to choose the consequence.

Independent Practice: The instructor will play the video of a man sharing his story about his journey in analyzing situations. YouTube: "I forgave my brothers killer | WALLO267 | TEDxBuckhead" https://youtu.be/wTNBx-iLkyo. The instructor will ask students if they can see parts of themselves in the speaker. Students will engage in a narrative writing activity to elaborate about being able to let go the feelings of revenge to prosper. Students will draw upon their past experiences to support their point. Students will evaluate the choices the speaker made prior to being incarcerated and the choices he is now making upon his release. Students will document responses in their workbook. Students will share out.

Lesson Wrap Up: Students will form a sequential restorative circle and answer what are some of the consequences of engaging in and not engaging in revenge?

*Challenge: Bring in an article or social media post of two music artists resolving a conflict without violence! Be prepared to summarize the steps taken to avoid the conflict.

Bonus El Mundo (The World)

Like most albums in Hip-Hop, the artist will give you bonus tracks or bonus content and this book will be no different! The phrase, history often repeats itself comes to mind when taking a look at this track. Back in September 2001, I was introduced to the track "What's going on" which included all the big names in Hip-Hop and R&B at the time: Destiny's Child, Nas, Puff Daddy, Mary J. Blige, Jermaine Dupri, Ja Rule, Eve, Questlove, Nona Gaye, Nelly, Alicia Keys, Nelly Furtado, N'Sync, and others. At the time I did not know it was a remake of the legendary Marvin Gaye track of the same name. When Marvin Gaye put out his version it was designed to uplift people in regards to the Vietnam War and Social Injustice. The 2001 version was initially recorded to bring awareness to the AIDS epidemic in Africa, but it was recorded days before the September 11th attacks, and it soon became a song about unity in the United States. It never fails when something catastrophic happens everybody comes together and it no longer matters what race they are or what social class they come from. We embody the "United" part of the United States in those moments.

The lyrical breakdown comes from the 2001 version from the artist Nas, when he states, "why his words forever remain dealing with these modern day problems" in reference to Marvin Gaye. In the year 2020, we are still asking what's going on when it comes to the Corona Virus Pandemic, Police Brutality, Sex Trafficking, School to Prison Pipeline, still Social Injustice, and Opioid Addiction. We are working out all the Social Emotional muscles here, but we are specially focusing on our interactions with others. We cannot control the events that are happening around us but we can control our actions to make things better. YOU HAVE GREATNESS INSIDE OF YOU! Why wait for something drastic to happen to showcase it? Shouldn't appreciating diversity, having respect for others, being socially engaged, and relationship building be the norm? I truly believe it should. We all need to have a mindset shift when it comes to our treatment and interactions with others, for only love can conquer hate.

LESSON PLAN FOR EL MUNDO

Materials Needed: Flip chart paper, pens or pencils, student's workbooks, and computers with internet access.

Objective: Students will train their RELATIONSHIP SKILL muscles by planning and participating in a Service Learning Project to help out the community. (**Skill –** SOCIAL ENGAGEMENT)

CCSS.ELA: RL.9-10.2 Determine a theme of a text and analyze in detail its development over the course of the text, including how it emerges and is shaped and refined by specific details; provide an objective summary of the text. W.9-10.3 Write narratives to develop real or imagined experiences or events using effective technique, well-chosen details, and well-structured event sequences. SL.9-10.1 Initiate and participate effectively in a range of collaborative discussions (one-on-one, in groups, and teacher-led) with diverse partners on grades 9–10 topics, texts, and issues, building on others' ideas and expressing their own clearly and persuasively.

Appetizer: What is the theme of this text?

Vocabulary: The instructor will review the vocabulary words. The instructor will ask for examples of each vocabulary word. Catastrophic- A sudden event that causes very great trouble or destruction. Engagement- The fact of being involved with something. Epidemic- A widespread occurrence of an infectious disease in a community at a particular time. Pandemic- A disease prevalent over a whole country or the world. Unity- The state of being united or joined as a whole. Uplift- To elevate or stimulate someone morally or spiritually.

Prior Knowledge- The instructor will ask students if they have ever done a nice deed for someone without expecting something in return.

New Knowledge- The instructor will state that helping others is a part of their personal growth. The instructor will inform students that their legacy is tied to how people remember them.

Guided Practice: Giving Back. The instructor along with the students will plan a Service Learning Project in the community. The group will decide on which day and time, preferably a Saturday or afterschool. The group will also decide on the activity. Potential events: cleaning up a park, assisting a retirement home, volunteering at a food pantry or soup kitchen, collecting items for the homeless, making and giving out sandwiches to the homeless, or volunteering with a home building project (depending on age of students). The instructor will be the project manager and reach out to the community organizations to schedule the event and to inform the parents of the students.

Independent Practice: Reflection. Upon completion of the Service Learning Project, students will write a one page paper about their experience. Students will document the place of the Service Learning Project, the activities they did, the people they met or interacted with, what impact their service had and how they felt about giving their personal time to help the community.

Lesson Wrap Up: What is one emotion you experienced during the Service Learning Project?

*Challenge: Participate in three (3) Service Learning Projects as a group during the school year.

REFERENCES

Buckner, J. C., Mezzacappa, E., & Beardslee, W. R. (2003). Characteristics of resilient youths living in poverty: The role of self-regulatory processes. *Development and Psychopathology*, 15(1), 139-162.

Buckner, J. C., Mezzacappa, E., & Beardslee, W. R. (2009). Self-regulation and its relations to adaptive functioning in low income youths. *American Journal of Orthopsychiatry*, 79(1), 19.

Busch, J. (2012). What is Hard Work? *Premier Magazine*. Retrieved from http://www.primermagazine.com/2012/live/what-is-hard-work

Center on the Developing Child. (2011). *Building the brain's "air traffic control" system: How early experiences shape the development of executive function (working paper no. 11)*.

Chetty, R., Hendren, N., Kline, P., & Saez, E. (2014). Where is the land of opportunity: The geography of intergenerational mobility in the United States. *Quarterly Journal of Economics*, 129(4), 1553-1623.

Core SEL Competencies. Retrieved from http://www.casel.org/core-competencies

Covey, S. (1989). *The 7 habits of highly effective people*. New York, NY: Simon and Schuster.

Denham, S. A. (2006). Social-emotional competence as support for school readiness: What is it and how do we assess it? *Early Education and Development*, 17(1), 57-89.

Diliberti, M., Jackson, M., Correa, S., & Padgett, Z. (2019). *Crime, violence, discipline, and safety in U.S. public schools: Findings from the school survey on crime and safety: 2017-18 (NCES 2019-061)*. U.S. Department of Education. Washington, DC: National Center for Education Statistics.

Durlak, J. A., Weissberg, R. P., Dymnicki, A. B., Taylor, R. D., & Schellinger, K. B. (2011). The impact of enhancing students' social and emotional learning: A meta-analysis of school-based universal interventions. *Child Development*, 82(1), 405-432.

Farrington, C. A., Roderick, M., Allensworth, E., Nagaoka, J., Keyes, T. S., Johnson, D. W., & Beechum, N. O. (2012). *Teaching Adolescents to Become Learners: The Role of Noncognitive Factors in Shaping School Performance—A Critical Literature Review*. Consortium on Chicago School Research. Chicago, IL.

Greenberg, M. T., Domitrovich, C. E., Weissberg, R. P., & Durlak, J. A. (2017). Social and emotional learning as a public health approach to education. *The Future of Children*, 27(1), 13-32. Retrieved from http://www.jstor.org/stable/44219019

Greenberg, M. T., Katz, D. A., & Klein, L. C. (2015). The potential effects of SEL on biomarkers and health outcomes: A promissory note. In Durlak, J.A., Domitrovich, C.E., Weissberg, R.P., Gullotta, T.P., & Comer, J. (Eds.), *Handbook of social and emotional learning: Research and practice* (pp. 81-96). New York, NY: Guilford Press.

Heick, T. (2019). 12 Barriers to Innovation in Education. *Teach Thought*. Retrieved from http://teachthought.com/the-future-of-learning/12-barriers-innovation-education

Jones, S. M., Barnes, S. P., Bailey, R., & Doolittle, E. J. (2017). Promoting social and emotional competencies in elementary school. The Future of Children. 27(1), 49-72. Retrieved from http://www.jstor.org/stable/44219021

Sklad, M., Diekstra, R., Ritter, M. D., Ben, J., & Gravesteijn, C. (2012). Effectiveness of school-based universal social, emotional, and behavioral programs: Do they enhance students' development in the area of skill, behavior, and adjustment? *Psychology in the Schools*, 49(9), 892-909.

Stauffer, B. (2020). What are 21st Century Skills? *Applied Education System*. Retrieved from http://www.aeseducation.com/career-readiness/what-are-21st-century-skills

Thompson, R. A. (2014). Stress and child development. *The Future of Children*, 24(1), 41-59.

Weissberg, R. P., Durlak, J. A., Domitrovich, C. E., & Gullotta, T. P. (2015). Social and emotional learning: Past, present, and future. In Durlak, J.A., Domitrovich, C.E., Weissberg, R.P., Gullotta, T.P., & Comer, J. (Eds.), *Handbook of social and emotional learning: Research and practice* (pp. 3-19). New York, NY: Guilford Press.

SONG NOTES

1. **Meek Mill (2012)** "Dreams and Nightmares" on the *Dreams and Nightmares* album.

2. **Dave featuring Burna Boy (2019)** "Location" on the *Psychodrama* album.

3. **DJ Khaled featuring Big Sean (2019)** "Thank You" on the *Father of Asahd* album.

4. **Fabolous featuring Charlie Murphy (2004)** "Church" on the *Real Talk* album.

5. **Fabolous (2011)** "Pain" on the *S.O.U.L Tape*.

6. **Jay Electronica (2009)** "Exhibit C" on the *Victory* mixtape.

7. **The Cool Kids (2009)** "Summer Vacations" on the *Gone Fishing* mixtape.

8. **Dave East featuring Styles P (2018)** "Beloved" on the *Beloved* mixtape.

9. **J. Cole featuring TLC (2013)** "Crooked Smile" on the *Born Sinner* album.

10. **Fabolous featuring Marsha Ambrosius (2009)** "Stay" on the *Loso's Way* album.

11. **21 Savage featuring Future (2016)** "X" on the *Savage Mode* EP.

12. **French Montana featuring Max B & The Weeknd (2017)** "A Lie" on the *Jungle Rules* album.

13. **Common (2005)** "Be (Intro)" on the *BE* album.

14. **Lil Wayne featuring Drake (2017)** "Family Feud" on the *Dedication 6: Reloaded* mixtape.

Index

Made in the USA
Monee, IL
02 March 2022

92113967R10052